A New **Reflection** Of Me

30 Affirmations to Build and

Cultivate Your Foundation of

Self Love

Tequila Myers

This book is available at quantity discounts for bulk purchases. For more information please contact:

www.tequilamyers.com
Tequila Myers
tequila@tequilamyers.com

DISCLAIMER:
The purpose of this book is to educate and affirm confidence. The author and publisher shall have neither liability nor responsibility for anyone with respect to any loss or damage caused directly or indirectly, by the information contained in this book.

Your success in building your foundation of self love is dependent upon, remaining positive, confident and serving yourself in your daily practices.

Printed in the United States of America

I dedicate this book to all women struggling with low self-esteem, self love and confidence. To the young girls and women who are trapped by society's definition of beauty, know that you are amazing in your own right and no one defines your beauty but you.

A New Reflection of Me

CONTENTS

Acknowledgments

Preface

ACKNOWLEDGMENTS

I want to first give thanks to God, our creator who has made all things possible for me. This journey called life is full of obstacles, detours, and delays, but there would be nothing to gain without those trials and tribulations. I'm humbled to know that I have been created, called and purposed to fulfill this work; it is my divine assignment here on earth. I am extremely grateful this opportunity and accept it with high honor.

To my honey, Mel, thank you for all of your support, patience, and understanding and most importantly for loving me, for me. I know I can be a handful but your strength keeps me grounded. Thank you for always reminding me of self determination. I appreciate all that you do for our family and I love you.

To my amazing, intelligent, beautiful, star-child Melanni, you are the reason I do what I do. Your drive and dedication to be the light that leads the way for others inspires me daily. Thank you for loving me and encouraging me to always be my best self because you were watching. I have achieved so many things, but you are by far my greatest accomplishment. Thank you for believing in me even when I didn't.

My family and friends, thank you for all your support, prayers, dedication, and standing by my side when I needed you most.

A New Reflection of Me

PREFACE

As a teen, I remember one of my mentors told me "The day you stop loving yourself, is the day you stop living". At that age I had no idea what she was talking about but for some reason that statement stayed with me. In my early twenties I thought about it again I acknowledged the truth in that statement but never really understood the power behind it. The magnitude of this statement would later ring true and echo in my head daily.

In today's society it's easy to become obsessed with our physical attributes and costly material things; instead of appreciating ourselves and celebrating everything that makes us beautiful internally and externally. Acknowledging everything about ourselves that not only make us unique, but also identifying our signature "thing". It can be the way you walk, talk, or that cute little dimple in your chin.

Redirecting our focus and intentionally practicing Self Love allows us to love ourselves so that we can open ourselves up to receiving love from someone else. When we love ourselves, we are happier and experience an overall sense of joy from that love. This serves us in a way that truly feeds our spirit from the inside, the way it should be. After all, our spirit lives and thrives on Self Love.

Thinking back on her words, although I didn't understand exactly what she meant by saying "that is the day you stop living"; as an adult I can now look back and read between the lines. The moment we stop loving ourselves, all value and worth are removed which leads to us believing that we are no longer deserving of anything good. That we don't deserve to be happy. This mindset is the most dangerous thing we could adopt for ourselves.

Increase the value in and of your life by sowing seeds internally to live a happy and more fulfilling life.

- TEQUILA MYERS

Introduction

Self love is the foundation on which all our morals, principals, and character are built. It is essentially the way we see and feel about ourselves; which also determines how we treat ourselves and others. Often times we get comfortable with hiding what we consider to be the ugly parts of ourselves and walk around covered in all the glitter and gold we can manage at once, knowing we don't feel all that pretty on the inside. Internally we are a huge ball of mess, but on the outside we look like a million bucks.

Having Self Love gives us strength to ignore the judgments and opinions of others, encouraging us to expose the not so beautiful parts of ourselves and ultimately embrace them. This not only allows us to accept and love everything about who we are, but the idea is to understand that as we continue to live, we will always be a work in progress.

I'm sure everyone understands by now that no one is perfect and all put together, all the time. So why are we trying to portray this about ourselves?

In this book are several I-centered affirmations that will help and add stability to your foundation of Self Love. Select a few and repeat them several times a day, every day, to transform your thinking and reprogram your mindset. So you can exude an energy into the universe to bring happiness, peace, and joy internally, so that you can radiate it externally in your everyday energy and attitude.

It is very important to understand how affirmations work. According to the Merriam-Webster dictionary, the definition of affirm is to say that something is true in a confident way. To show a strong belief in or dedication to something such as an important idea. In other words, you are declaring this idea to be true to yourself and the universe.

Repeating these phrases changes your thoughts. You are creating a mindset that allows you to attract and manifest your desires in abundance.

The key to affirmations is to change your thinking. It's almost as if you are manually reprogramming yourself, intentionally providing a feed of positive thoughts to your psyche, multiple times a day, on a consistent basis. Repetition is key; constant exposure to positive thoughts allows the mind to grasp the concept, making it easier to understand, believe, and follow through with. Disregard negative thoughts and reinforce positive ones. Every day wake up with the expectation that you will have a great day.

Encourage yourself, after all it starts within you.

-Tequila Myers

A New Reflection of Me

4

ABOUT THIS BOOK

I wrote this book to help you build, cultivate, and nurture your foundation of self love - one day, month and year at a time. You'll do this by creating positive thoughts within your mental space daily. My hope is that with each affirmation you really look deep within to see how you can improve that specific area of your life with intentional thought and action.

I had one thought consistently when writing this book and that was empowerment. For this book to serve that specific purpose for either you- the reader, and for you to take a moment out of your day to return the favor and empower someone in your life. This book was designed to be a gift that keeps on giving, so take something from it, even if only one affirmation and share it- on social media, with a loved one, your girlfriends, or even a stranger on the subway. When sharing on social media please use include #anewreflectionofme.

Anytime you undergo a transformation, self work is required. That is why I included the self evaluation questions. These questions were designed to provoke thought and encourage you to recognize how your experiences have influenced your life, but most importantly your inner thoughts and how you feel about yourself. Doing the self work is what will allow you to live on purpose, elevate your thinking, have more control over your thoughts, and continue to strengthen your foundation of Self Love.

This is not just another motivational book or your average affirmations book, but more so a way to be transparent with yourself. A way to get naked in your thoughts and on paper to build yourself up without fearing judgment from others. My hope is that this serves as a reference guide for self reflection, to measure yourself and the progress you'll make. Regardless of your age or where you are in life, I am confident this book will help renew your mind and thoughts, to renew you.

If you are ready to do the self work it takes to transform your mind and build a stable foundation of self love; grab your journal or notepad, a pen and a few highlighters (for the really juicy ones). Get prepared to rebuild and strengthen yourself by pouring back into you.

Together we will elevate your confidence, self-esteem, and self-worth so that you can walk and stand tall in it every single day. Now is your time to stop dimming your light and shine like the bright, beautiful, star of a woman you are.

LIFE IS NOT PERFECT AND NEITHER AM I

Often times, as women we are so used to being in control that it can be difficult to just go with the flow and let the chips fall where they may. We get caught up in trying to be perfect and live the perfect fantasy life we've created in our heads. This causes unnecessary stress and madness in our households. We have to learn how to let go of thinking that life is perfect and we have to be perfect too.

Life isn't perfect and neither is man, never has been and will never be. That is the biggest mistake we make, trying to be perfect, and I consider this to be committing an act of violence on ourselves. Simply put, it's unhealthy and can have a multitude of negative effects on our emotional and mental state as well as our progress in life. It's time to stop seeking perfection in ourselves and in life because that is a treasure that will never be found.

What perfectionist ideas do I need to let go of in my life?

_____

_____

_____

_____

_____

_____

_____

_____

How has this way of thinking held me
back from accomplishing my goals?

_____

_____

_____

_____

_____

_____

_____

_____

What can I do to practice letting go of those ideologies?

_____

_____

_____

_____

_____

_____

_____

_____

I BELIEVE IN MYSELF AND SO DO THOSE AROUND ME

It's one thing to say you believe in yourself, but it is another to declare it with passion and actually believe it. Truth be told we have to be our biggest cheerleaders, if we have faith and believe in ourselves our peers are sure to follow. So, remind yourself of this daily. Ingrain it into your thoughts. Make it your life script.

When we truly believe in the value we bring to the world a mind shift happens that dismisses fear and gives us the courage to execute. This influences the way you feel about yourself and pushes you to keep going.

That is when courage and fearlessness changes our aura which allows us to attract people and opportunities that are in alignment with our dreams and goals. They believe in us, because they know that we believe in ourselves to keep going and accomplish our goals.

What do you believe about yourself?
Who are you?

_____

_____

_____

_____

_____

_____

_____

_____

How do you affirm what you believe about yourself?

_____

_____

_____

_____

_____

_____

_____

_____

How do others show their belief in you?

_____

_____

_____

_____

_____

_____

_____

_____

I CHOOSE TO BE HAPPY IN ALL AREAS OF MY LIFE

Happiness is one of the few things we have control over in our lives. Yes, life is life and we have various things and people involved that each plays a role in our every day interactions. Our families, careers, hobbies and so many other things are demanding more of us so eventually we stretch ourselves thin and we lose track of our happiness. Then, slowly we begin to feel stressed out, overwhelmed, and spin out into a complete mess. We cannot do this anymore. It's time to choose happiness at home, in the office, and every other aspect of your life.

Life happens, but don't get so caught up in life that you forget to be happy. Circumstances are temporary and can change at any time. Understanding that you have a choice to create the happiness you want is where it starts. Remember, it's the tough times that shape your personality and character making you the fabulous woman you are today. If you want it claim it! Don't forget to take time and treat yourself to a salon visit, a manicure, or even a walk in the park alone to enjoy some you time.

17

What is my definition of happiness?

_____

_____

_____

_____

_____

_____

_____

_____

What are some things I can start doing to celebrate my happiness?

_____

_____

_____

_____

_____

_____

_____

_____

How can my life change as a result of
making a conscious choice to be happy?

_____

_____

_____

_____

_____

_____

_____

_____

NO ONE LOVES ME MORE THAN I LOVE MYSELF

When you love yourself you act and treat yourself in a way that shows self respect, dignity and integrity; you automatically demand the respect of others. People will treat you the way they see you treat yourself. This is something I instill in my daughter every day.

Self love is almost magnetic in the way that it seems to attract the right relationships. Not only that, you can't love someone else, if you don't love yourself first. When you love yourself on purpose, you in turn show others how to treat you and love you. Don't give yourself -or anyone else for that matter- the green light to devalue or take away your love for you. If you love yourself first, you won't ever feel the need for anyone else to fill that void.

How do you practice self love?

_____

_____

_____

_____

_____

_____

_____

_____

What are some things that you
absolutely love about yourself?

_____

_____

_____

_____

_____

_____

_____

_____

What are your standards/boundaries
when it comes to how others treat you?

_____

_____

_____

_____

_____

_____

_____

_____

I ACCEPT EVERYTHING ABOUT MYSELF JUST AS IT IS, KNOWING THAT I AM UNIQUE

You are one-of-a-kind. No one has what you have. No one else is exactly like you. No one on this earth has your smile. It is all yours. We were all sculpted, molded, hand-crafted, in a way that our beauty is solely our own. Each created with a unique and tailored set of features, characteristics, and purpose that cannot be fulfilled by anyone but you.

Own everything about you, from head to toe. Learning to accept our strengths, weaknesses, including areas of improvement, flaws and all is what makes us beautiful. That is what makes you stand out in a crowded room. That is what attracts people to you. That is why you are special!

What unique characteristics or traits do you possess that make you special?

_____

_____

_____

_____

_____

_____

_____

_____

What flaws have you acknowledged and accepted about yourself?

_____

_____

_____

_____

_____

_____

_____

_____

What do others compliment you on the most?

_____

_____

_____

_____

_____

_____

_____

_____

EVERY DAY I LIVE TO BE THE BEST ME

I look at each day as an opportunity to create a better version of me than I was yesterday. As a new chance at life. Starting the day with this mindset creates an optimistic perception which focuses on the possibilities versus the impossibilities. Instead of having the mindset of "I can't", I take the mindset of "how can I" accomplish my goals for today, even if it's not a major goal.

A simple mindset shift can take your life from ordinary to extraordinary. When you operate from a place of "I can" you learn to expect things to work in your favor. So as you work on yourself, you expect to see change. Your expectations of improvement will not only hold you accountable, but will also allow you to see opportunities to grow with clarity, making the self work much easier.

What actions can I take everyday to be my best self?

_____

_____

_____

_____

_____

_____

_____

_____

How will I hold myself accountable to taking these actions?

_____

_____

_____

_____

_____

_____

_____

How can I shift my mindset to be more
of the change I want to see?

_____

_____

_____

_____

_____

_____

_____

_____

I HAVE THE POWER TO HEAL MY HEART AND MY SPIRIT

As women we are nurturers and caregivers by nature, but we sometimes forget about our healing powers. We act quickly to heal someone else, but when we need healing we either fail to recognize it or won't make time for it. This has to stop. How can we be of any good to our families, friends, or careers if we are not taking the time to heal ourselves?

Experiencing hurt and heartbreak can send anyone into a downward spiral, even the strongest woman. We have to remember that we also can heal ourselves just as we heal others. This is where loving you and being consistent in recognizing when healing is necessary comes in. Many times it's as simple as venting to a girlfriend and other times it requires a great deal of effort and self work to heal our hearts and spirits. Whatever experience, past or present that is causing you pain should be considered an open wound that needs healing.

How has hurt and heartbreak affected
your spirit and what have you done to
release the pain?

_____

_____

_____

_____

_____

_____

_____

_____

Who or what in your life plays a big role in healing your spirit?

_____

_____

_____

_____

_____

_____

_____

How do you heal your spirit when you feel down and out?

_____

_____

_____

_____

_____

_____

_____

I AM CAPABLE OF DOING AND ACHIEVING ANYTHING I WANT

Every now and then we can all use a reminder to help us get back on track, whether we've been a distraction to ourselves or distracted by someone else. That reminder means knowing our capabilities and acting on them accordingly. Consider why you wanted to set this goal for yourself in the first place and let that motivate you.

If you've set your heart out to do something whether it's going back to school to earn your degree, living a healthier lifestyle, becoming more spiritually connected or any other goal you've set for yourself. You can achieve it as long as you consistently remind yourself that you can do it and the reason why it's important to you. Sometimes we have to challenge ourselves to achieve our goals.

What do you desire to do or achieve in your life?

_____

_____

_____

_____

_____

_____

_____

_____

How can you avoid distractions and stay on track with your goals?

_____

_____

_____

_____

_____

_____

_____

_____

What serves as your reminder to why
you set your goals? What is your why?

_____

_____

_____

_____

_____

_____

_____

_____

TODAY, I WILL BE AT PEACE WITH MYSELF, THE UNIVERSE AND EVERYTHING AROUND ME

Being at peace with you is something money can't buy. It's invaluable and priceless. It's an indescribable feeling, but one I encourage everyone to experience. It starts with acceptance of yourself, and then you move into forgiveness. First, accept all of your character flaws, emotional imperfections and shortcomings. Then you forgive, not only those who've wronged you, but forgive yourself for all of the broken promises you made to yourself.

Those around us, sense that peace in our aura. Exuding that peace into our surroundings gives a supercharged boost to that internal peace and happiness, producing genuine and authentic joy in our lives. Peace fosters joy, joy encourages confidence, and confidence gives us wings.

What comes to mind when you think of being at peace with yourself, the universe and everything in your life?

_____

_____

_____

_____

_____

_____

_____

_____

Where is your place of peace?

_____

_____

_____

_____

_____

_____

_____

What are some things you do to
maintain your inner peace?

_____

_____

_____

_____

_____

_____

_____

I DEFEAT MY CHALLENGES, THEY DO NOT DEFEAT ME

Adversity in some way is common to us all, however the way in which we choose to react to it- is what defines us. Those are the experiences that make us who we are. Every lesson whether good or bad, big or small, presents an opportunity to grow. Some challenges though, are harder than others and the opportunity or benefit we have to gain can be easily overshadowed by the obstacles we encounter in life.

Don't let that fool you or discourage you. Use these moments as stepping stones- on your journey to a better, stronger woman. You are more brave, resilient, and heroic than you know. Our trials may be tough, but victory is always near. Every lesson learned along the journey will only make the celebration more worthwhile.

List some encouraging words that help you overcome challenging moments.

_____

_____

_____

_____

_____

_____

_____

_____

What challenges in your life have given you the most strength?

_____

_____

_____

_____

_____

_____

_____

How do you feel after defeating a challenge?

_____

_____

_____

_____

_____

_____

_____

BALANCE IS MY KEY
TO LIFE

Let's face it; balance is something we all struggle with. Whether you're a working mom, entrepreneur, or adopting a new lifestyle change, it seems like a never-ending hurdle trying to create balance in our lives. It took me a long time to understand that I could not split my time and energy evenly all the time. I had to face the harsh reality that some things will get neglected at times and it's okay, but I learned it's how I juggled the most important things in my life to maximize your time effectively is what really matters.

Finding that perfect place of balance doesn't happen overnight, it takes time and practice. You'll have to adjust here and there when things change in your life but once you've gotten the process down, it will get easier every time. Try not to be so hard on yourself, you are not alone, everyone has experienced this struggle before.

What does having balance in your life look like?

_____

_____

_____

_____

_____

_____

_____

_____

Do you have a structure system to help maintain your balance? Explain.

_____

_____

_____

_____

_____

_____

_____

_____

What chores/duties can you delegate to
create flexibility in your life?

_____

_____

_____

_____

_____

_____

_____

_____

I AM FABULOUS, AMAZING, BEAUTIFUL AND COMFORTABLE IN MY OWN SKIN

YOU ARE BEAUTIFUL!

Yes, I said it and I meant it. As women, we are constantly being fed subliminal messages about what the standard of beauty is. Failing to realize that beauty is in the eye of the beholder. Every part of you is beautiful; your eyes, your smile, your curves, your personality, and most importantly your heart. You are beautiful because YOU are YOU. No one else can define your standard of beauty and you should never give anyone permission to.

Remind yourself of this every day. In fact, I challenge you to do just that. Look in the mirror every morning for the next seven days and tell yourself, I am fabulous, amazing, beautiful, and comfortable in my own skin. Don't just say it believe it, and when you say it, smile your best smile.

What do you consider to be your most
beautiful features? (interior and exterior)

_____

_____

_____

_____

_____

_____

_____

_____

I challenge you to create your own
morning mantra to celebrate your
beauty. Write it below.

_____

_____

_____

_____

_____

_____

_____

What makes you feel sexy?
(certain clothing, person, place, thing)

_____

_____

_____

_____

_____

_____

_____

_____

I CAN DO ANYTHING, IF I DO IT WITH CONFIDENCE

Confidence and self-assurance shows that you are certain in what you are saying or doing. It's a feeling or belief in ones power, ability, or value. Having confidence in yourself gives you the power to perform at your highest level. It's not only a feeling, but an energy you exude. When others sense your confidence it commands attention in an indescribable way.

Owning your confidence comes with many benefits, most importantly it cultivates self pride and self worth. Therefore, you can easily recognize your strengths and capabilities so you can begin to act on them with greater confidence in yourself. Being confident not only improves and feeds your self-esteem, but it also sets you up for success.

What is your definition of
confidence and how important is
it to you?

_____

_____

_____

_____

_____

_____

_____

_____

List three ways you own your confidence?

_____

_____

_____

_____

_____

_____

_____

_____

How has your confidence increased your self-worth?

_____

_____

_____

_____

_____

_____

_____

_____

MY DIVINE ASSIGNMENT WAS PURPOSED FOR ME

We are all deserving, each and every one of us. God doesn't love me or anyone else more than you. We are all given equal love, grace, mercy, and deliverance. Each and every one of us has a pre-ordained purpose and destiny, if we choose to listen and be obedient to the process. That is key.

Just as we see others walking in their journey of purpose, we too have an assignment crafted especially for us. It goes back to listening and being obedient to the process. Life presents itself in many ways and eventually things will begin to happen for you and your life will take on a certain direction that leads you on the journey to your assignment. When the time comes, be ready to accept it wholeheartedly and with intentional action.

What do you feel is your divine assignment on earth?

_____

_____

_____

_____

_____

_____

_____

_____

If unsure, what are you passionate about?

_____

_____

_____

_____

_____

_____

_____

_____

What do find yourself doing most that you enjoy?

_____

_____

_____

_____

_____

_____

_____

_____

I POSSESS INFINITE POTENTIAL

As human beings we all have unlimited potential. Anything we choose to focus our minds on can be manifested in our lives. We only experience limited thinking when we overcomplicate and try to perfect things, when nothing was meant to be perfect. You have the ability to think, be creative, and do anything your heart desires. That alone confirms your potential. Once you adopt this belief, you release the need for permission from anything or anyone to validate you or your potential.

This may sound simple, but a thought is behind every great idea that has made an impact in the world or in our lives personally. Recognizing that potential and the power it holds is like a bird expanding its wings to fly for the very first time. It provides a sense of freedom and awareness that serves as a catalyst for you to conceive, birth, and make your dreams an everyday reality.

What potential do you recognize within yourself?

_____

_____

_____

_____

_____

_____

_____

_____

How are you or how can you begin to maximize your potential?

_____

_____

_____

_____

_____

_____

_____

What do you expect to gain as a result of acting on your potential?

_____

_____

_____

_____

_____

_____

_____

_____

CHANGE IS CONSTANT IN LIFE I, CAN ACCEPT THAT

Things change every day, nothing stays the same forever. Everything and everyone around us changes every single day. We all advance through different phases of life causing us to grow and learn more about ourselves and the world around us. Change is inevitable whether we like it or not.

Being open and accepting of change affects your perception and allows you to see the positive versus the negative. Instead of seeing it as change, look at it as growth or an opportunity to grow. Shifting your mindset opens your mind to see the opportunity to learn or add another experience to your resume of life instead of seeing the challenge in stepping out of your comfort zone. Change is certain this we know for sure, and is necessary to advance to the next level no matter what your position in life. Will you grow from it or use it as a crutch to make excuses?

What changes can you be more accepting of in your life?

_____

_____

_____

_____

_____

_____

_____

_____

How has your changing perception affected the way you see change and how has it helped you?

_____

_____

_____

_____

_____

_____

_____

What changes have been the most challenging to accept and what have you learned?

_____

_____

_____

_____

_____

_____

_____

I HOLD THE POWER IN MY LIFE

You have more power and control over your life than you may think. You have the power to decide your environment, actions, the things and people you allow to be in your life. If it's not serving you in the way it should, you have the power to let go and keep moving. You are the chief activator of change in your life at all times. The moment you decide that you cannot activate change in any aspect of your life, is the moment you decide to give up your power.

Any statement that does not affirm your power is a declaration of powerlessness. Believing that you have no power or control is dangerous to your emotional health and can leave you hopeless and stuck. Take control of the power you possess and stop allowing others to be dictators when they are merely spectators in your life. They haven't earned the power, so why are you giving it to them?

List some things/people that you will take your power back from and why.

_____

_____

_____

_____

_____

_____

_____

_____

What are you going to do with that power to change your life?

_____

_____

_____

_____

_____

_____

_____

Create an affirmation that reminds you
to stand in your power every day.

_____

_____

_____

_____

_____

_____

_____

_____

I EXPECT NOTHING BUT THE BEST FOR MYSELF

Why settle for less when you can really live the life you want? Not only should you want it, but you should expect it. When you expect something, you anticipate it; that anticipation should come to life in your persistence, drive, and consistency toward the expected outcome. This means that your actions are in alignment with your expectations. Faith without works is dead. You have to be active in what you expect no matter what it is.

This speaks to both your personal and professional life. You can't expect to be a great mother or wife without a plan. It may not be a grand plan, but if you have told yourself that you are going to do certain things that you believe will help you achieve that, you have a plan. Also, you can't expect to advance in your career or become an entrepreneur without a strategy or plan to do execute. So remember, it's all about aligning your actions with your expectations so you can live and be your best self.

What expectations do you have of yourself personally or professionally?

_____

_____

_____

_____

_____

_____

_____

_____

List your expectations in order of importance to you.

_____

_____

_____

_____

_____

_____

_____

_____

What actions can you align with your
expectations to get your desired result?

_____

_____

_____

_____

_____

_____

_____

_____

EVERY MORNING I WAKE UP TO ANOTHER CHANCE AT A NEW BEGINNING

Yesterday has passed; who says tomorrow can't be different? Just because you were in the midst of a storm yesterday, your circumstances can change today. Take advantage of the opportunity to reinvent yourself. To change your life and work toward something meaningful. Every day is a chance to recreate the life you want.

Don't let another day pass without making a conscious decision to take a step in a new direction and create a new beginning for yourself. Another opportunity to change. Another chance at living the life you want. Every morning you should wake up with the understanding that you have to seize and conquer the day to make it what you want. Create your new beginning.

It's your life. You are the creator, executive producer, designer, and director.

What will you do differently today than you did yesterday?

_____

_____

_____

_____

_____

_____

_____

_____

How will you take action everyday to
continue in the direction you chose?

_____

_____

_____

_____

_____

_____

_____

What advantages do you see in
everyday being a new opportunity?

_____

_____

_____

_____

_____

_____

_____

_____

I HAVE BUILT MY LIFE ON A SOLID FOUNDATION OF PEACE, JOY AND LOVE

Inner peace and self love are both priceless. You can't truly have joy without peace and love. Having a strong foundation can have so many positive effects on your life; most importantly your perception of yourself but it also affects how others perceive you. When your foundation is strong, you can't be shaken and no one can influence your peace, joy and love. It's firmly planted like the roots of a tree and serves your need for stability and strength in your life.

Those around you can also automatically see and feel that you are rooted in something that makes you strong. They can feel it, and naturally, they want to know how you got it. They want it because they know everyone doesn't have it. Doesn't it feel good knowing that you do?

What is your definition of peace, joy and love?

_____

_____

_____

_____

_____

_____

_____

_____

How do you celebrate the peace, joy and love you've created in your life?

_____

_____

_____

_____

_____

_____

_____

_____

What people or things contribute to this area of your life on daily basis?

_____

_____

_____

_____

_____

_____

_____

_____

IT IS NEVER TOO LATE TO FORGIVE MYSELF FORGIVENESS IS MY LIBERATION

Forgiveness is a gift to you; it has nothing at all to do with the other party involved. Without seeking closure through forgiveness, you continue to hold on to things that slowly eat away at you and ultimately affect your quality of life. Once you understand this, so many things in your life become clear. You experience maturity, gain wisdom, and understanding like never before. You also heal wounds, new and old, by taking a step in the direction to liberate yourself from that unnecessary baggage.

When you learn to forgive yourself and others, you learn that you no longer have to carry the burden and baggage that kept you tied down with unhealthy emotions. You learn to stop blaming yourself for things that you have no control over. Look in the mirror and say everything you forgive yourself for.

What mistakes have you made that you need to forgive yourself for?

_____

_____

_____

_____

_____

_____

_____

_____

What have you learned as a result of forgiving yourself?

_____

_____

_____

_____

_____

_____

_____

_____

How can you use this experience to heal
yourself and become a better you?

_____

_____

_____

_____

_____

_____

_____

_____

LIFE IS BEAUTIFUL AND I ALLOW MYSELF TO SEE THAT

Our everyday schedules usually keep us with a full plate, right? I say "schedules" because we stick to them as if we have been programmed to do these things day in and day out. Sometimes we have to stop and smell the roses. That can be something as simple as taking a moment to sit still and collect your thoughts in peace. Personally, I like to enjoy a nice sunset or to sit out on the front porch looking at the moon.

Life is beautiful in so many ways if we only would stop for a moment to take a look. Think about your children or anything you hold dear to your heart. Seeing and experiencing the things we love is almost magical. Nature and nurture both influence my life in so many ways and to me, that's what makes life beautiful.

Create a schedule below with days and times for your alone time?

_____

_____

_____

_____

_____

_____

_____

_____

What is your idea of stopping to smell the roses?

_____

_____

_____

_____

_____

_____

_____

_____

List three things that you can or will do to celebrate your alone time?

_____

_____

_____

_____

_____

_____

_____

_____

TODAY I REPLACE MY ANGER WITH PATIENCE, UNDERSTANDING, AND COMPASSION

Sometimes we hold on to things from our past experiences that don't serve us in our current place in life. Often times, this is how we develop anger and negative attitudes. When we do this, it does us more harm than good. Whether its childhood trauma, past relationships, or broken promises we've made to ourselves, we have to learn to let go. Yes, these experiences contributed to your journey, but they don't have any control over your future; only you control your destiny.

Life is about learning to have patience, understanding and compassion, anger is not a healthy emotion. Replace anger with something positive that deposits back into you; to live in a place of peace, free of any and everything that may be limiting your life.

What are you holding on to that doesn't serve you in your current place in life?

_____

_____

_____

_____

_____

_____

_____

_____

How have those experiences influenced your life?

_____

_____

_____

_____

_____

_____

_____

_____

List three things from your past that can be beneficial to you in the future? Why?

_____

_____

_____

_____

_____

_____

_____

_____

I AM THE ARCHITECT OF MY LIFE AND USE LIFE LESSONS AS MY TOOLS

Life is a set of building blocks, with our life lessons being the tools that help build our foundation. Your role in that process is being the chief architect. Being the chief architect in your life means that you play a major role in how it's designed. Equipped with the tools and experiences you've earned over your lifetime gives you an advantage to create the life you want and deserve. They will serve as your guide to creating the ideal structure for your life and spirit to reside in.

Understand that these are not final plans or "the blueprint", they can be pretty close, but there is always room to make necessary changes along the way as you grow and learn more about yourself. You are in charge to create, build, direct and design the life you want to live while enjoying the journey of life.

How are you using your life tools to create a better life for yourself?

_____

_____

_____

_____

_____

_____

_____

_____

What life lessons have been the most influential?

_____

_____

_____

_____

_____

_____

_____

Without these lessons what do you
think your life would look like?

_____

_____

_____

_____

_____

_____

_____

_____

I AM READY TO CHANGE

In order to truly transform your life you have to be ready for change. That often requires sacrifice. There is no such thing as doing the same thing over and over, expecting change in your life. Your mindset has to align with your vision to get to the place in your life that you desire. Expectations have to be set. Action has to be taken. You may even have to give up some things that are not conducive to the new direction of your life.

Change can look different for us all, whatever that looks like for you, begin to work towards it today and repeat it daily. Remind yourself that you can do this. Believe it or not, you have the power of change over your future, if you choose to take charge. Let your dreams guide you to that place of change today so you can live out your dreams tomorrow. Align your actions with your vision to be the change you want to see.

What can you change or improve within yourself or your life?

_____

_____

_____

_____

_____

_____

_____

_____

What are you willing to sacrifice to activate change in your life?

_____

_____

_____

_____

_____

_____

_____

What actions will you take to make those improvements?

_____

_____

_____

_____

_____

_____

_____

_____

I AM RESPONSIBLE FOR MY ATTITUDE AND EMOTIONS, EVEN WHEN I WANT TO BLAME OTHERS

It can be easy to blame others for how we feel. Honestly, no one can dictate our emotions but us. Taking responsibility for our actions and the roles we play is the first step in building better lives and futures. Owning up to those shortcomings allows you to see the areas where growth and maturity are needed most.

After taking responsibility, the next step is to get a better understanding of how to recognize what causes those emotions and triggers those changes in attitude. When you know what it is, you can work through it until it no longer affects you. Your commitment and accountability to be more responsible and in control of your emotions will be a rewarding experience as it will influence other areas of your life.

How do you take personal responsibility for your attitude and emotions?

_____

_____

_____

_____

_____

_____

_____

_____

List three triggers that impact your
attitude and emotions? How do you
keep yourself in check?

_____

_____

_____

_____

_____

_____

_____

_____

What will you do to avoid blaming
others for your actions the way you feel?

_____

_____

_____

_____

_____

_____

_____

_____

I AM A SHINING BEACON OF INSPIRATION AND EMPOWERMENT

Are you the person that uplifts the room by simply being present? We've all experienced this, whether you are that person or know someone like this. There's a certain feeling you're left with after such an experience. I believe that we all have that within us; being a beacon of light to inspire and empower others could be yours. We each shine in our own way and that light shines brightest when we feel that strong sense of empowerment.

Never allow anyone or anything to cast a shadow over that amazing thing that you possess, that light. Dimming that light doesn't serve you or those you were meant to serve and influence. It shines bright for a reason, serving as a magnet to those in need of uplifting. Your light could help guide someone out of a dark and lowly place. Never dim your light, it was meant to shine.

How do you empower and inspire those around you?

_____

_____

_____

_____

_____

_____

_____

_____

Name three individuals that have inspired or empowered you?

_____

_____

_____

_____

_____

_____

_____

What was it about them that influenced you?

_____

_____

_____

_____

_____

_____

_____

_____

NO ONE CAN GET IN THE WAY OF MY DREAMS EXCEPT ME

Fear, perfection, and comparison are your biggest enemies. They are infamous for being opportunity snatchers and dream killers. They work against progress and cause limited thinking, forcing you into a mental space of believing that you aren't enough. That you aren't worthy or don't deserve what's rightfully yours. This is what stops us from living out our dreams.

Let go of fear and give yourself permission to do whatever you desire. Ignore that inner perfectionist and be satisfied with doing your best. Stop comparing yourself to anyone else because you don't know what they've gone through to get there. Learn to get out of your own way so that you can be bold and live your dreams out loud.

What are some things you can do to get
out of your own way so that you can
live out your dreams?

_____

_____

_____

_____

_____

_____

_____

_____

In what ways do you compare yourself to others?

_____

_____

_____

_____

_____

_____

_____

How has fear played a role in you not
taking action to live your dream?

_____

_____

_____

_____

_____

_____

_____

_____

MY LIFE JOURNEY IS AN INFINITE PATH OF GROWTH

The journey of life is a process, one not meant to be understood from a simplistic perspective. However, we should pay close attention because it helps us to get a better understanding of who we are. The experiences and the lessons are all key components that play a role in our story. Those lessons stretch us, make us uncomfortable, and encourage us to grow and develop the strength to become more resilient.

As your journey continues you receive new tools that equip you for the next lesson. It's natural to anticipate and desire to have control over our experiences. Yet, the mystery of not knowing forces us to learn and look deeper within ourselves for the answer. This not only adds to the perspective of understanding ourselves on a deeper level, but it also allows us to grow every day as we go on this journey.

What has been your most memorable life experience?

_____

_____

_____

_____

_____

_____

_____

_____

How have your experiences influenced your perception of life?

_____

_____

_____

_____

_____

_____

_____

_____

What experiences have encouraged you to grow the most?

_____

_____

_____

_____

_____

_____

_____

_____

JOY IS THE FRUIT THAT FEEDS MY SPIRIT DAILY

Many people confuse joy and happiness with being one in the same. While they are both emotions, they are very different and we experience them on different levels. Happiness speaks to a feeling of contentment and satisfaction; this is often a temporary experience since it happens as a result of something. It's also subjective to the experience, such as feeling happy after doing something you enjoy.

Joy holds more weight, because it's a more intense heartfelt emotion, an internal feeling that's connected to your spirit. It's more realistic and long-lasting, unlike happiness it's not dependent upon external circumstances such as the things we experience every day. Joy is a feeling of being connected, an attitude of your heart. When enduring life's most difficult challenges, it is joy that feeds our spirit and delivers us through. Let joy be the fruit that feeds your spirit daily.

What is your definition of joy?

_____

_____

_____

_____

_____

_____

_____

_____

List three moments when joy helped you through a difficult time.

_____

_____

_____

_____

_____

_____

_____

What activities do you practice to fill your spirit with joy?

_____

_____

_____

_____

_____

_____

_____

_____

CONCLUSION

The process of affirming yourself is similar to planting a seed that will someday bear fruit which you will harvest and enjoy. To do this, it has to be provided the proper growing conditions to flourish. The seed serves as the positive thoughts that you are planting within yourself daily.

The fruit to be harvested is the growth, confidence, understanding and self love that you will gain as you experience the journey. The soil plays an important role in the outcome of the harvest. The soil must be rich; full of vitamins and nutrients to produce good fruit. Your spirit is the soil that will house and grow this seed so it must be kept and well taken care of.

When planting your seed keep in mind a shallow hole is not capable of growing a strong tree. The cultivation process is continuous and essential to fostering the growth and transformation that you desire to achieve. Just as you prepare soil for planting, we have to prepare our spirits to stretch and grow.

This means being intentional in the actions you take to care and prepare for your tree to bear fruit. When cultivating your seed it is important to maintain the expectation that it will thrive. Setting these expectations early also makes you ready to receive. Now that you have planted your seed and began to water it daily, it is time to watch that seed grow. Speaking these affirmations to yourself several times a day is you watering that seed.

Nurture and protection are also important for an optimal harvest. When the sprouting process begins there are several factors to consider such as environmental elements, threats, and other deterrents. Maintaining care for your spirit means that you are not only feeding your mental and emotional needs, but your physical health needs as well.

Finding ways to decrease stress levels, eating healthy, and sustaining your overall well-being is part of the nurturing process. Our environment plays a key role in how we nurture and feel about ourselves; make sure your environment serves you. Protection is equally necessary. Without protection birds, squirrels, and other animals may can come and harvest your fruit before it has matured or ripened enough causing shock and possibly affecting the future growth of additional fruit in the future.

The same goes for our Self Love and confidence. If it's not protected, we leave ourselves susceptible to the interruption or destruction of everything we've worked so hard for. This can have effect on us, but our future generations as well. Protect your Self Love and confidence from anything or anyone in your space.

After planting your seed, cultivating it, nurturing it, protecting it, and watching it grow, the harvest has come. You have taken the time to build yourself up from the inside out, which is no small feat. Celebrate. This is the season to reap what you have sown back into yourself. The seed you planted has bore the fruit of maturity, patience, and clarity into your life because you wanted it and took the action to make it happen.

Just as you can experience the journey of a seed to the time it bears fruit, you can experience internal growth and happiness by affirming yourself consistently to cultivate and nurture your foundation of Self Love.

ABOUT THE AUTHOR

Tequila Myers, CEO of Perpetual Growth Institute and Brand Confidence Academy has always been an avid reader and writer. As a young child who suffered from a speech and language disorder she often wrote poetry and short stories as a way to express herself.

She believes that writing has helped her not only overcome the disorder, but has also helped to boost her confidence when speaking on the stage.

As an empowerment speaker and business coach, Tequila understands the power of using ones voice and the influence that comes with it. She developed Perpetual Growth Institute to help women gain clarity around and discover their purpose to build powerful and influential brands by monetizing their message.

A graduate of Franklin Covey Leadership Academy with over 10 years in IT communications and marketing, she has adopted several unique strategies for building business acumen, managing projects, and creating business processes that maximize productivity and efficiency.

Tequila currently lives in Oklahoma with her husband, daughter and family dog. When she isn't wearing one of her many hats she's probably sewing, cooking, volunteering in the community or completing her latest DIY project. For more information or to book Tequila to speak at your next event, visit tequilamyers.com.

The following pages have been left blank to write a few of your own personal affirmations that you've created. Please share them on social media using **#anewreflectionofme** and on Tequila's fan page at facebook.com/tequilamyers.

Cheers to creating a new reflection of you!

Photo credit: Shelia Johns

_____

_____

_____

_____

_____

_____

_____

_____

_____

_____

_____

_____

_____

_____

_____

_____

_____

_____

_____

_____

_____

_____

_____

_____

_____

_____

_____

_____

_____

_____

_____

_____

_____

_____

_____

_____

_____

_____

www.ingramcontent.com/pod-product-compliance
Lightning Source LLC
LaVergne TN
LVHW040053090426
835513LV00027B/293